Original title:
Windows to the Future

Copyright © 2025 Creative Arts Management OÜ
All rights reserved.

Author: Vivian Laurent
ISBN HARDBACK: 978-1-80587-030-2
ISBN PAPERBACK: 978-1-80587-500-0

Whispers of Coming Ages

In a toaster, sprites dance tight,
Crispy dreams in morning light.
Jellybeans with wings do fly,
Sipping soda as they sigh.

Future cats in rocket boots,
Bouncing high on rainbow zoots.
Tickles sent from cosmic beams,
Pajamas filled with giggly dreams.

Sparks in the Fog of Time

Frogs in top hats play charades,
Futures mixed with sugary shades.
Juggling time, they spill the beans,
Sipping lemonade from machines.

Teleporting to the moon,
Dancing to a silly tune.
Banana peels on hoverboards,
Laughs that echo, cutting chords.

Manifestations of Promise

Flying bikes with silly grins,
Riding streets while time spins.
Pizza pies that scream and shout,
Futures filled with cheese and clout.

Giant gummy bears take flight,
Waving paws with pure delight.
Candy rainbows paint the sky,
Watch the popcorn factories fly.

Gifts Wrapped in the Future's Glow

Unicorns in hula hoops,
Dance around in silly loops.
Confetti stars in crazy hats,
Eager squirrels with fancy bats.

Ninjas made of jellybeans,
Sneak around in playful scenes.
Time machines in funky shoes,
Bringing joy with every cruise.

Chasing Tomorrow's Light

I peered beyond the curtain's edge,
Where laundry flaps like flags of a pledge.
Tomorrow's sun grins at a silly chance,
While squirrels plot their acrobatic dance.

My coffee spills, the cat takes a leap,
Waking the dreams I've tried to keep.
I wave at the future, it blinks back at me,
As blinkers mark time in a rush to be free.

Breaching the Veil

Through the sheets I spy a new ruckus,
The dog's chasing shadows and making a fuss.
A world full of giggles, where puppies reside,
And kittens build castles on dreams that collide.

Be careful, I say, don't trip on the air,
For laughter is dancing, it's everywhere!
The couch is a rocket; we're heading to Mars,
With snacks for the journey and bright candy bars.

Illumination of New Beginnings

With a wink, the toaster starts its spin,
Bagels inspired to wear a new grin.
Under the glow of the fridge's hum,
Tomorrow whispers jokes — oh, here they come!

The clock gets busy turning seconds to gold,
While plants gossip secrets they've never told.
A parade of ideas marches through my mind,
Wrapped in a ribbon that's brightly designed.

Spectrums of Change

Colors splatter against the old wall,
A rainbow brigade is ready to haul.
With crayons and laughter, each stroke feels right,
As scribbles take flight through the starry night.

Socks become puppets looking for shoes,
In this carnival chaos, we choose our muse.
With bubbles in pockets and giggles on hand,
The future is sparkly, wild, and unplanned!

Glimmers of Tomorrow

In the kitchen, gadgets gleam,
A robot cooks and starts to beam.
It burns the toast, but what a show,
A dance-off with the pasta, oh no!

Flying cars above my street,
Clucking chickens with two left feet.
A future bright with coffee spills,
And laughing at our techie ills.

Beyond the Glass

Peering through a digital sheen,
A cat in shades looks quite serene.
She scrolls through memes as time flies by,
With hopes of fish and pizza pie.

Potted plants with Wi-Fi rage,
Debating which is the best page.
They leaf through apps, they're quite absurd,
No one knows if they've heard a bird.

Ports of Possibility

With a click, the future beams,
A squirrel dreams of laser schemes.
He builds a jetpack out of twine,
To steal his neighbor's lunch divine.

In this realm, socks dance at night,
While jellybeans take wing in flight.
Who needs a plan? Let's have some fun,
With time machines that won't outrun.

Visions Unfolding

I see a world of snazzy phones,
Where fish hold meetings on their moans.
The cow jumps high to reach the sky,
While robots pause for a quick chai.

Futuristic bikes with wings so grand,
Make every ride a wild bandstand.
With laughs galore and hiccuped cheer,
Each day is wacky, never drear.

Fractals of Possibility

A cat in a hat, off to the space,
Riding on bacon, oh what a race!
Wormholes of laughter, twist and they twine,
Future's a riddle, and I'll take my time.

Jellybean rockets, zooming so high,
Singing their songs beneath cotton candy sky.
Unicorns giggle, as time does leap,
Chasing the moments, both silly and deep.

Embracing New Horizons.

A penguin in pajamas, dance on the beach,
Sipping on smoothies, within arm's reach.
Making new friends, like a seal with a hat,
Life's just a circus, oh look at that!

Flying fish sailboats, on marshmallow seas,
Tickling the clouds, with a whiff of cheese.
All of our dreams, like balloons in the air,
Float with delight, without any care.

Glimmers of Tomorrow

Electric snails move at lightning speed,
Wearing green goggles, they giggle and plead.
Pizza-flavored comets, chase after the sun,
Wishing on sprinkles, everyone's fun!

A t-rex on a skateboard, grinding with style,
Twinkling and flashing, making us smile.
Banana peels slip, but laughter's so nice,
With each little mishap, we roll like dice.

Portals of Possibility

Dancing goldfish, wearing sparkly shoes,
Swinging on chandeliers, they spread silly news.
Rainbows with umbrellas, skip puddles of cheer,
Funny and fearless, no reason to fear.

Chocolate chip mountains, come take a bite,
Silly time travelers, turn day into night.
With each giggle shared, worlds twirl and spin,
Let's open our hearts, let the fun begin!

The Infinite Possibility

In a world where cats wear hats,
And dogs discuss philosophy,
A robot brews our morning tea,
While we chase dreams of harmony.

Flying cars park on the trees,
As aliens drop by for tea,
They say, 'Earth's a zoo, don't you see?'
With cosmic jokes for all to spree.

An octopus plays the trombone,
With jellybeans for his fans,
Together they dance with joy,
In a land made of candy plans.

So let's embrace this wacky ride,
Through paradoxes, jokes, and glee,
For in each twist and turn we find,
A giggle at infinity.

Chasing Tomorrow's Glow

Time-traveling squirrels in bow ties,
Gathering acorns for the year,
While we toast with cups of slime,
Laughing as we shed a tear.

Flashy shoes that help us float,
Skipped ahead to next week's bash,
With disco balls that sparkle bright,
And a DJ made of mashed potatoes' stash.

There are penguins running the show,
Teaching us how to slide and spin,
In this wacky world we roam,
Dancing underneath our skin.

So grab your hat and join the fun,
Roll with the punch, don't be shy,
For the glow of laugh-filled tomorrows,
Always captures the curious eye.

Preludes to the Evolving

Evolving turtles with smart phones,
Hunting for memes in the park,
As gophers pitch their radical plans,
To revolutionize the dark.

Chickens coding in computer labs,
Making apps for the coolest games,
While frogs host wild online talks,
All while avoiding the blame.

Funky robots with funky hair,
Roll out ideas, bizarre and bright,
In a world where weird is king,
And logic takes a backseat at night.

So let the laughter guide our path,
As progress meets the silly twist,
For in this dance of what might be,
The future's a comical mist.

Signs of the Imminent Shift

The sun flips pancakes for breakfast,
While shadows play hopscotch in glee,
A penguin pops out from the clouds,
To declare it's time for jubilee!

Weird creatures jive down the street,
With harmonicas made of cheese,
While ocelots in tuxedos sing,
A serenade to the swaying trees.

Time is but a rubber band,
Stretching dreams beyond the realm,
While squirrels in capes take command,
In this whimsical, nutty helm.

So grab a snack and join the ride,
The shift is here, so take a seat,
For laughter is the guiding light,
As we embrace the absurd beat.

Foresight in the Framed

I peer through the frame, what do I see?
A cat in a hat, sipping tea with a bee.
Pigeons are dancing, quite the charade,
Life is a circus, but the windows won't fade.

Future's a riddle, with secrets to find,
A cow on a scooter, imagination unlined.
Chickens in tuxedos, they waltz on the lawn,
Through each funny glimpse, a new day is born.

Dreams Beyond the Sill

A squirrel in sandals, planning a trip,
With chips on his shoulder, he starts to flip.
Past the old shutters, the oddities waltz,
Dreams in bright colors, no reason to halt.

An octopus juggles, while birds sing out loud,
With laughter and joy, oh it feels like a crowd.
The moon dons a tutu, my heart starts to race,
In the frame of my window, there's magic in space.

The Glass that Divides

Is that a pop tart? No, a cozy surprise,
A toaster is dancing, in front of my eyes.
It flickers and toasts, with a whimsical fling,
Through this glass divide, such joy it will bring.

A dog in pajamas, he dreams of the skies,
With visions of biscuits, and pies that won't lie.
Oh, the laughter and joy, as stories unwind,
In this glimmering glass, the future's so kind.

Journeys Through the Looking Frame

I take a quick peek, oh what do I see?
A giraffe on a tricycle, as bright as can be.
Around him, a parade of cakes with a grin,
Through this quirky portal, let the fun begin.

A cow in a rocket, zooming past stars,
With a pig in a cape, oh how bizarre!
Each journey unfolds, with giggles to spare,
In this magic frame, there's a joke in the air.

The Light Brightening Over the Dunes

The sun peeks shyly, a cheeky grin,
Casting shadows where dreams begin.
Sandcastles rise with great ambition,
Only to tumble with slight derision.

Kites dance wildly in the brisk air,
Waving at seagulls without a care.
Beach balls bounce, a joyful delight,
As sunblock warriors prepare for a fight.

Footprints in sand fade away,
But laughter lingers, here to stay.
Crispy fries and sandy toes,
Life's sweet moments, everyone knows.

As the day fades with a chuckle or two,
We pack up our dreams and our picnic stew.
The twilight beckons, playful and bright,
Inviting more giggles to take flight.

Frames of Dreams Yet to Flourish

In a gallery of giggles, stories waltz,
Each frame whispers secrets, never false.
The paint spills stories, a rainbow spread,
With laughter spilling, like buttered bread.

A cat in a hat says, "What's the fuss?"
Teacups are waltzing, who made the mess?
Pictures speak louder than words ever could,
With snickers and snorts, it's all understood.

Clouds of cotton candy float on by,
In a world where unicorns learn to fly.
Each stroke of the brush brings joy combined,
Where every giggle is blissfully designed.

We'll frame our follies, our blunders too,
Each moment a treasure in vibrant hue.
In this quirky museum of silly delight,
Our frames of dreams shine brilliantly bright.

Glances at Tomorrow's Brushstrokes

Peeking through time with a twinkle of eyes,
We chase after futures that wear silly ties.
Hilarity reigns as we sketch and draw,
Unpredictable twists, leaving us in awe.

The moon plays tricks, wearing silly hats,
While pigs take flight with sassy spats.
Brushstroke giggles dance across the page,
As flowers in tutus strike a pose on stage.

What will tomorrow hold, we jest and muse,
Will gophers wear sneakers or sing the blues?
Canvas of chaos, bright colors collide,
With paint that splatters our joy bona fide.

In this carnival of dreams unplanned,
We'll pirouette through futures, hand in hand.
So come take a glance, let laughter ignite,
In the bright, zany spectacle of life's twilight.

The Horizon Beckons

A telescope aimed at the sky,
Where aliens wave and unicorns fly.
The clouds are made of cotton candy,
And the sun's a giant disco, oh so dandy!

With each new dawn, a wild surprise,
A three-legged dog wearing glasses, oh my!
Future held in a cheeseburger bun,
Life's a carnival, let's have some fun!

Looking Through Time's Lens

Peeking through a kaleidoscope view,
A talking cat sings the blues for you.
Back in the past, a dino does jive,
While robots hum tunes, we come alive!

Time-travel trousers, we bounce and leap,
To dance with the stars while the world sleeps.
Each tick of the clock brings laughter and cheer,
Jokes from the future make us pee with fear!

Frames of Tomorrow's Dream

In a world of bubbles, we skip and glide,
Where laughter's our guide and joy our ride.
Painted rainbows on pickle-flavored toast,
Silly hats on llamas we love the most!

Jumping through frames of cartoon delight,
Giggling fish dance under the moonlight.
Here, socks have personalities that gleam,
And bread sings songs in a whimsical dream!

Portals of Potential

Jump through the portal, you're in for a treat,
Parrots in tuxedos serve ice cream on the street.
Jellybean flowers sprout up on demand,
And time-traveling ants form a marching band!

Each twist and turn unveils a new game,
Unicorns at parties treat all the same.
Laughs echo brightly through each crazy night,
As we paint our futures with colors of light!

Dimensional Glimpses

Through a hole in the wall, I peeked in,
Saw a cat in a hat, doing yoga with kin.
Time-traveling squirrels played poker and danced,
While singing the blues as they boldly pranced.

An alien chef cooked pancakes on Mars,
Serving them up in his fleet of sleek cars.
With syrupy stardust and cosmic delight,
Breakfast up high felt just out of sight.

The sun wore sunglasses, lounging in rays,
While clouds hosted parties, igniting new ways.
Jellybean rain fell with a colorful cheer,
Turning the mundane into laughter and beer.

In this zany realm where giggles can fly,
The future's a playground, just don't ask why!
For laughter leads pathways, wide open and bright,
And every silly twist brings delight into sight.

Insights at Dawn

Birds schmoozing over coffee made from stars,
Chirping their secrets of traveling cars.
While squirrels with glasses investigate dreams,
Finding odd answers in reality's seams.

Morning breaks open with a dance of the bold,
As sunlight spills stories we've never been told.
Frogs croak in harmony, wearing bow ties,
While butterflies gossip about last night's surprise.

Cereal boxes sing as they pour out their charm,
Milk floats in updrafts, it won't do any harm.
A toaster belches toast in a comedic way,
Bread flying high into the brightening day.

So here we sip wisdom in mugs full of cheer,
With laughter and nonsense as our souvenirs.
In a world that's unfolding, let's grin and explore,
Each dawn is a chance to open new doors.

Reflections of an Emerging Era

Mirrors show me dragons wearing silly hats,
And fish playing chess with ice cream for cats.
Time keeps on ticking, yet dances a jig,
As robot comedians tell jokes about big.

On the avenue, neon flamingos parade,
While octopuses juggle in colorful charades.
Balancing spoons, they laugh with delight,
As squirrels and raccoons throw a raucous night.

With bubbles that float filled with giggles galore,
Happiness blossoms on every front door.
So let's trade our worries for whispers of fun,
In a realm where the oddity has just begun.

As this world spins forward, let's leap with a cheer,
For life is just a party, come join in my sphere!
With every new dawn, let's relish the quirky,
For future is painted in joy, never murky.

The View Beyond Today

Through kaleidoscope lenses, we catch a bright glance,
As jellybeans tango in a vibrant dance.
Skyscrapers giggle, wearing whimsical hats,
And pigeons in suits plan their business chats.

Today folds away like an old wrinkled sock,
While laughter unfurls in an unending clock.
Monkeys on bicycles zoom past with glee,
Delivery robots dressed up as a bee.

In a park full of wonders, each leaf is a friend,
Where giggles and chatter dash around every bend.
With marshmallow clouds and rainboots on frogs,
All limitations dissolve like old soggy logs.

So wave to the skyline where odd things can play,
Embrace every moment, ignite the relay.
For tomorrow is waiting with whimsy to show,
The view beyond today is a comic tableau!

Visions Beyond the Glass

Peering out, I see a cat,
Wearing shades, how about that?
It dances with a funky beat,
While typing on a tiny seat.

Flying fish ride on a bike,
Bubblegum trees, take a hike!
A clock that ticks in reverse so bold,
Wishes made from jelly and gold.

Thinkers with hats made of cheese,
Contemplating life's little tease.
Who knew that ducks could recite?
Their quacks, well, they're pure delight.

So let's raise a toast to the odd,
In a world where logic's a fraud.
Through glass, we see life's silly tune,
Join the laughter, life's a cartoon!

The Keyhole to Infinity

Here's a keyhole, what do we see?
A llama in a hammock, sipping iced tea.
It dreams of galaxies made of pie,
And swims in chocolate clouds in the sky.

An octopus running a shoe store,
Selling sneakers to a dinosaur!
With laces that dance and colors so bright,
They moonwalk together under the moonlight.

Bunnies in bow ties all gather 'round,
Debating on who wears the best crown.
With carrot cake as their subject of choice,
Each nibble approving, they cheer and rejoice.

So peek through the keyhole, take a glance,
Life's absurd, we must take a chance.
Embrace the wacky, the odd, the divine,
In this quirky realm where laughter will shine!

Pathways of Tomorrow's Light

Bouncing on clouds, a squirrel's delight,
Twirling pickles in the pale moonlight.
With roller skates on their furry feet,
It's a party where laughter can't be beat.

Candy canes growing tall like trees,
Singing to the rhythm of the breeze.
A rainbow slide to zip and zoom,
Who knew joy could sprout in bloom?

There's a robot offering hugs all day,
While juggling cupcakes in a bright ballet.
Each bite a joke, each laugh a song,
As we skip through paths where we all belong.

So take a step down this fun-filled road,
Where whimsy's the currency and joy is bestowed.
In the glow of tomorrow's dazzling light,
Let's dance with glee from morning till night!

Fragments of the Next Chapter

Turn the page, reveal a sight,
A penguin juggling with all its might.
Dressed in a tux and glasses so cool,
It heads to school, it's nobody's fool.

Pancakes with legs prance about,
Chasing syrup and yelling out.
In a world where food can run and play,
Breakfast becomes quite a wild display.

Frogs in hats hosting a fair,
Selling umbrellas that float in the air.
With tunes played by frogs on a stage,
They make every moment feel like a page.

So flip that book, watch it unfold,
In this realm where nonsense is gold.
Fragments of laughter, a chapter trying,
In the land of the silly, we find we're flying.

The Horizon's Promise

Through the glass we peek ahead,
Chasing dreams that dance instead.
Maybe next year we'll all be stars,
Or just sitting in our cars.

Lattes flying, papers too,
Dancing robots, all brand new.
What's that now? A pizza drone?
If it's late, we'll call the phone!

Flying pigs and sunny skies,
Our wild hope just makes us sigh.
But hold on tight, let's skip the fuss,
Our future's here, it's riding a bus!

Tomorrow's laughter, today's delight,
Magical gadgets that shine so bright.
With smiles and giggles, off we zoom,
In this zany future room!

Shadows of Progress and Change

In shadows where the jokes collide,
The future's winking, oh what a ride!
Umbrella drones, just flipping high,
Avoiding rain, oh me, oh my!

Dogs in hats and cats in ties,
Smartphones that plot and sage advice.
Texting jokes to our own reflection,
Critiquing our outfit selection!

Coffee cups that sing with glee,
While old tech feels like a flea.
We giggle as we chase the trend,
Hoping our laughter never ends!

Oops! There goes my smart car's door,
Off it scoots to the neighbor's floor.
Clowning into the future's embrace,
With silly shadows we keep pace!

Vistas Beyond the Present

Peeking through the crystal pane,
Seeing cats with jetpack gain.
Fanciful sights that rise and fall,
Is that a pickle flying? Y'all!

Rainbow paths and neon lights,
Dancing robots on Fridays nights.
With giggles loud and joy inside,
This whimsical future, what a ride!

Unicycles zoom with flashy flair,
Wearing capes like they just don't care.
Poodle parades on hoverboards,
What a world! Who needs awards?

Our photos flash—a celebration,
Of silly dreams, a wild sensation.
Laughter echoes, pure and true,
In these vistas, we break through.

Projections of What Could Be

Gazing far on screens so bright,
Future jokes that take a flight.
Spinning tales of cheese and fun,
While robots join us, everyone!

Hover plants and singing trees,
Ticklish clouds that dance with ease.
Waffles talking in soft rhymes,
Absurd futures feel like chimes!

Taxi llamas, what a sight,
Riding home in pure delight.
Let's paint the world in quirky hues,
With laughter, joy, and lots of blues!

As we frolic through this place,
We flip our hair and set the pace.
In projections that swirl and be,
Together, forever, in jubilee!

Breaths of the Uncharted

Peering through glass, what a sight!
Nose pressed so hard, it feels right.
Squirrels plotting new mischief schemes,
While I sip my tea and daydream.

Tomorrow's jokes are waiting wide,
Like socks that waited for the ride.
Will my toast land butter-side down?
I'll laugh either way, wearing my crown.

What's outside, a gift or a glitch?
A garden gnome that starts to twitch?
With each breath, a chance to start,
A tickle of joy, captured heart.

So here I stand, at life's grand show,
Gazing far into the glow.
With every chuckle, a new quest,
Open the door, let laughter jest.

Reflections of What Lies Ahead

Mirrors of life, where the chaos swirls,
I catch a glimpse of future girls.
Dancing canines in tutus bright,
While I ponder if I'll take flight.

Time-traveling pets, oh what a thrill,
Riding through space on a giant dill.
I giggle at thoughts of all that might be,
Wishing for pickles that talk back to me.

A rooster in shades, rockin' the scene,
Cracking the code of a time machine.
Next week will this all make sense?
Or just be a splendid pretense?

With each tick-tock, absurd dreams race,
In my mind's eye, I see a hamster face.
As laughter tumbles, hope floats anew,
Future's a comedy, I'm laughing with you.

The Next Step Unfolds

Step right up, the circus awaits,
A trampoline bounce to leap through gates.
Every misstep leads to delight,
As I pave my path, what a hilarious sight!

A kangaroo jumps, offers a ride,
Waving at clouds like a sailor with pride.
Flipping through pages of quirky tomorrows,
Filled with giggles and joyful sorrows.

Twirling confetti, life's silly dance,
Who knew the future would start with a glance?
Magic tricks from a jester's hat,
Making me wonder, how about that?

Fingers crossed for surprises ahead,
A microwave wizard? Oh, just misread.
With each step, I twirl and spin,
The next great caper, let the fun begin!

Chambers of Infinite Potential

Hidden in rooms where the oddballs dwell,
A cactus in sneakers, weaving its spell.
What's in that box labeled 'Do Not Peek'?
A parade of sock puppets, oh, what a freak!

Frogs with top hats choreographing tunes,
I'm twirling with dreams beneath cartoon moons.
Each chamber whispers, "What's your delight?"
Loading up giggles, let's take flight tonight.

Anticipation grows like a sprout,
Wishing that one day we could just route.
Teleporting jellybeans, oh what a shock,
Crunching the numbers, or just the clock!

Here's to the mishaps that make us whole,
Searching for joy is a vigorous role.
So open these doors, come laugh with me,
In chambers that bumble with pure glee!

Bridges to New Beginnings

Wobbly planks across the streams,
We all walk on our daydreams.
Each step a giggle, a chance to trip,
Hold on tight, or lose your grip!

Cats chase shadows, dogs chase tails,
We share the road with fishy gales.
All dressed up in mismatched shoes,
Sailing off with silly views!

Join the dance on this rickety path,
Make a splash, unleash your laugh.
Every stumble, a comedy show,
Where tomorrow's mischief starts to grow!

With each step, a silly song,
In this world where we all belong.
Bridges beckon, let's skip and hop,
Onward we go, we'll never stop!

The Scope of What Is Yet to Be

Peeking through our misty glass,
What if jellybeans grow on grass?
A world where socks get up and dance,
And chickens learn to take a chance!

Flying fish on wheels, oh my!
Dancing donuts in the sky.
We'll ride on clouds made out of cake,
In futures bright, who needs a brake?

Every day, a wacky quest,
Searching for the silliest jest.
Who knew a squirrel could teach us flair?
As we explore without a care!

Tomorrow's dreams flip like pancakes,
Fuzzy logic and giggly mistakes.
What's next? A race with sleepy bears?
Endless laughter fills the air!

Vows to the Horizon

With a wink and a cheesy grin,
We make our promises with a spin.
Dare to dream, even when it's odd,
We'll have a giggle, odd or flawed!

I promise to wear my socks askew,
And share my ice cream with the zoo.
To dance like no one's watching me,
And sing in tune with the buzzing bee!

A sprinkle of joy, a dash of fun,
Together we'll shine like the midday sun.
We'll chase the clouds, soar with the breeze,
Laughing loud, with total ease!

To the horizon, our hearts we'll throw,
With silly vows, we'll steal the show.
Adventurers bold, let's start the race,
In this grand life, we've found our place!

Luminous Guides to the Unknown

Starlit pathways made of jello,
Following sparks of a bright yellow.
Glow-in-the-dark squirrels lead the way,
In this kooky night, come what may!

With toast-shaped maps, we've got it made,
Navigating the frosted brigade.
Slipping on laughter, tumbling bright,
Is this the way? Let's take flight!

Each corner turned is a surprise,
A dance with fate beneath the skies.
With each step, a silly rhyme,
Chasing dreams, oh what a climb!

Glow globes guiding through every twist,
We march to the heartbeat of the mist.
Together we'll shine, come join the fun,
In this dance, we are all one!

Hopes Carried in Shifting Winds

Balloons with dreams spin and sway,
Floating high on a breezy day,
Chasing clouds that wear a grin,
Who knew hope could dance with the wind?

A kite named 'Future' flops and flies,
Its tail caught in the neighbor's fries,
We laugh as it loops, then dives,
In laughter, our silly hope thrives.

The sun sneezes, then beams so wide,
While squirrels play hide and seek outside,
Each gust brings a chuckle or two,
What a wild ride for me and you!

So let's sail on this quirky breeze,
With dreams that beg to twirl and tease,
As long as we keep our spirits light,
We'll glide through the ever-spinning night!

The Path Less Walked

There's a trail that zigzags through the park,
Paved with giggles, it leaves quite a mark,
Each step a dance, each stumble a cheer,
Our footsteps echo, 'Let's go, my dear!'

Mismatched shoes and a fashion faux pas,
Laughter erupts as we're lost in the spa,
Finding treasure in each silly blunder,
In this crazy journey, we laugh as we wander.

We meet the cats, with their judgmental stares,
Offering wisdom as they groom their hairs,
While clouds toss confetti from above,
Each misstep is a sign of our love.

Together we leap, and together we fall,
On this wacky path, it's a ball after all,
We'll skip into sunsets, hand in hand,
Living life splendidly, oh isn't it grand?

Celestial Portals to New Beginnings

A creaky door to a bright new realm,
Where dancing stars take over the helm,
They twinkle and giggle, a cosmic parade,
Waving to us: 'Here's the fun we made!'

Space bunnies hop on meteors bright,
Telling tales of their dance every night,
Rabbits in space with sunglasses on,
Disco balls spinning, the boredom is gone!

In this galaxy of quirky delights,
Each hiccup is a dance under moonlight,
So grab a comet, let's ride into fun,
Shooting for laughs, one by one.

With stardust sprinkled upon our hair,
We'll twirl in mirth, without a care,
Beyond the stars, our dreams take flight,
In this hilarious cosmos, everything's bright!

Dreams Hovering Beyond the Present

A whimsical dreamboat floats on by,
With jellybean sails and a taffy sky,
We row with laughter, oars made of cheese,
Chasing dreams that giggle in the breeze.

The moon winks as we navigate,
Past marshmallow islands, a sugary state,
Each ripple of hope is a song untold,
Bubbling up laughter as our dreams unfold.

The compass spins, alerting the crew,
To magical realms where surprises accrue,
Sipping dream juice from mystical cups,
Toasting to moments that never give up.

So let's sail on until we can't stop,
With a sprinkle of joy and a jolly hip hop,
For each wave of giggles that sweeps us away,
Paves the legacies of our silly play.

Reflections of Paths Untaken

Oh look, a fork, I took a left,
But should have tried the right instead.
I found a cat, wearing a vest,
Now he won't stop dancing, I'm misled.

At crossroads, one might see a sign,
It says 'Go back! Not that way, friend!'
But on I trudge, in my own line,
Where squirrels hold court till the day ends.

I met a man who sold me dreams,
He charged me in odd change and puns.
His magic beans were just baked creams,
Yet somehow, life feels more like fun!

With every step I take, I laugh,
Through tangled paths of whims and wit.
I guess my compass is a giraffe,
Leading me on without a permit.

Navigating the Unseen

I walked a road marked 'Do Not Enter',
With signs that squawk like agitated birds.
My GPS gave up, just a mentor,
Said, 'Keep it vague, use your own words!'

I tripped on dreams, fell through a gate,
Where daisies wear hats and sing with glee.
I asked a frog about my fate,
He just croaked, 'Laugh, it's all free!'

A busker strumming on an old shoe,
Plays tunes that tickle the clouds above.
He stops to wink, says 'Join the queue!'
As picnic ants play drums with love.

Now I dance under umbrellas of cheer,
Navigating traps laid by luck's own hand.
Life's a circus, and oh dear,
Who knew I'd run with a marching band?

Hints of the Unfolded

Peeking at tomorrow, what a sight,
Bubbles of laughter float by like dreams.
Confetti comes down in bright delight,
As I chase cats that plot and scheme.

A magic hat holds all my plans,
A rabbit laughs, says 'Not today!'
He pulls out donuts, and flops like a fan,
Says, 'Let's eat first, then push play!'

Chalk drawings come alive at night,
Tickling the stars with stories bold.
A dance-off starts under the streetlight,
Where wishes are traded and tales are told.

Each hint I catch is just a tease,
Like jello that wiggles but won't quite set.
The future may be weird, I can't appease,
But I'll keep on laughing, no regrets!

The Soundtrack of Yet to Come

My playlist's wild, it's quite a mix,
With polka, jazz, and some odd quirks.
A marching band of clowns plays tricks,
While butterflies plot some funky works.

The kettle sings a catchy tune,
As toast does a little tango on its plate.
Sprinkles on cupcakes make me swoon,
Each bite's a party, never late!

The echoes of laughter fill the air,
As koalas blog about their day.
They strum on lyres, without a care,
Saying, 'Join the dance, come what may!'

With every note, a new surprise,
Tomorrow's melody waits to play.
Each silly moment comes in disguise,
Making life a song that leads the way.

Seeds of Unseen Growth

In gardens where the daisies bloom,
A snail races towards its doom.
Each seed a tiny wish to sprout,
Yet all they do is just pout.

With whispers of the sunny days,
They plot to grow in silly ways.
Some sprout up high, and others low,
But all agree they steal the show.

A squash that thinks it's quite a peach,
A pumpkin who just wants to beach.
They laugh in rows, a silly sight,
And dream of tall and wild moonlight.

So here's to all the seeds we sow,
May laughter be what helps them grow.
In cracks and crevices they play,
And cheer us on to brighter days.

Catalysts of Change

A cat with goggles on its head,
Declared itself the smartest bred.
Figuring out how to take flight,
While falling down just feels so right.

With time machines made out of forks,
They journey through the land of storks.
Each funny twist brings endless fun,
As fruit flies plot their wild run.

Ideas mix in bubbling pots,
Like socks that dance in silly slots.
A shuffle here, a wiggle there,
Is that a mouse? Just playing fair!

So let the ruckus all unfold,
With giggles that we can behold.
In chaos lies the sweetest change,
Where laughter leads, and plans feel strange.

Illuminated Paths Forward

A flashlight stuck on silly mode,
Is dazzling quite the funny road.
Each beam a dance, a joyous flic,
As shadows chuckle and go thick.

With neon signs that point and blink,
They guide us closer to the brink.
Of understanding how to glide,
On slippery paths, we slip and slide.

A bubble wand can show the way,
When life feels heavy like a tray.
Pop! The path reveals a laugh,
As clouds applaud and join the chaff.

So follow light with carefree glee,
As laughter shapes our destiny.
Through twists and turns, we skip and prance,
Embracing every wobbly chance.

Directions of the Yet to Come

With paper maps all upside down,
We navigate this silly town.
A compass points to ice cream shops,
To tasty treats that never stop.

Turns out we lost the way back home,
But isn't getting lost the fun?
With giggles shared, we roam and run,
As life's an ever-changing pun.

An arrow made of silly string,
Directs us to the joy we bring.
With every step, we twirl and leap,
Creating memories we keep.

So let's embrace the paths we roam,
With laughter tracing every dome.
The future's bright, so full of cheer,
Adventures wait and soon appear.

Through the Looking-Glass of Withheld Days

I peek through a glass, what do I see?
Cats in top hats, sipping sweet tea.
A dog playing chess, with a glance so sly,
Winking at squirrels who flutter on by.

A rabbit in sneakers, running so fast,
Yelling, "Move it, folks! We've got to have a blast!"
The clock strikes a tune that makes everyone dance,
As the flowers sing ballads of chance after chance.

Jellybean rain falls from skies made of cream,
While turtles on skateboards all giggle and beam.
Life's just a circus, it's quite the charade,
With rhythm and laughter, I'm totally swayed.

This looking-glass world, oh, what a delight,
Where dreams live in colors, so vivid and bright.
If you've got a whimsy, just let it take flight,
In the land of the silly, it's all just so right!

Shimmering Skies Ahead

Up in the clouds, I see penguins fly,
Wearing shades and umbrellas, oh my, oh my!
They slip on the rainbows, like skateboards of cheer,
While monkeys on clouds serve pineapple beer.

The sun shines like disco, all glitzy and gold,
As the chickens all dance, and the roosters get bold.
With socks in the air, they gather in packs,
Singing karaoke and cracking their backs.

I spot a big whale, dressed up as a queen,
Twirling and spinning, so fancy, so keen.
The stars twinkle back with a wink and a grin,
As laughter echoes in my sky-high spin.

So here's to the skies, where the silly won't cease,
With dancing delight and a sprinkle of peace.
In shimmering shades, all the colors collide,
In this merry spectacle, my heart's open wide!

A Doorway to the Unwritten

I found a doorway with a sign that said 'Fun,'
A portal to stories yet to be spun.
It creaked as I opened, what treasures inside,
A ride on a snail, or a hotdog slide!

A cat in a cape smirks, 'Welcome aboard!'
With unicorns, cupcakes, and a giant board.
The laughter erupts, as we sail through the air,
Balancing pizzas while riding a bear.

Crayons and sprinkles fill up the whole room,
As everyone scribbles in colors that bloom.
A dance-off begins; it's a sight to behold,
With gorillas in sequins who break out in gold!

To canaries that rave, I join in the spree,
This doorway leads wild, so come on, let's see!
No limits, just laughter, no rules to confine,
There's a story for all, so let it be thine!

Tides of the Coming Dawn

The sun dips down low, while jellyfish sway,
And mermaids do cartwheels in the bay.
With flip-flops and laughter, they splash in the tide,
Chasing the rainbows with giggles beside.

A walrus in shades plays the saxophone right,
As octopuses dance in the dimming twilight.
With surfboards of toasts, they ride the wave's crest,
Laughing and hollering, they're having the best!

The moon starts to wink, giving stars a cue,
As turtles roll by in a hula routine, too.
The tides whisper secrets of dreams and delight,
In a world painted vibrant, from day into night.

So let's join the party, just dance and be free,
In the tides of a dawn that's just waiting to see.
With a sprinkle of joy and a tickle of fun,
Our adventure awaits; it's just barely begun!

An Opus of Anticipation

Peering through glass, I see the clocks,
Future's a puzzle, with missing locks.
My cat wears a hat, quite absurdly grand,
She might just rock a band in cartoon land.

Ducks in top hats waddle and quack,
Telling me secrets from days I lack.
A sandwich in space does a flip or two,
Maybe tomorrow, I'll join that crew.

Martian dance parties, so wild, so free,
With aliens teaching their moves to me.
As I take a leap through the funhouse door,
I tripped on my shoe, but I laughed for sure.

The future's a stage, with puppets and cheers,
Even my toaster is brewing some beers.
In this wild ride where logic takes flight,
I'll order a pizza from galactic height.

Letters to Tomorrow

I sent a postcard to my own next week,
It said, 'Dear Future, don't be so bleak!'
Received a reply, crabby yet bright,
'Quit asking about me, I'm busy tonight!'

Pigeons in bow ties deliver my mail,
While fish in a fountain regale their tale.
'Tomorrow's a circus,' the dolphins said,
With cotton candy clouds above a big head.

I wrote a haiku on a chipmunk's back,
Hoping to find where reality's at.
It scampered away, wearing my thoughts,
Dancing around like it knew a few knots.

So here I am, sipping tea with a broom,
While the future giggles and dances in gloom.
Got plans to meet robots at quarter to five,
But first, let's check if my mailbox's alive.

Dreams Delivered by Light

I ordered a dream online yesterday,
With virtual unicorns to lead the way.
The courier fumbled, lost in a loop,
Delivered me joy in a giant scoop.

I rode on a comet, fast as a beam,
With pizza and ice cream, the perfect dream.
A raccoon in sunglasses sang me a tune,
While whirlwinds of jellybeans filled the room.

Tomorrow's in slow-mo, with hiccuping stars,
Even the sun wears funky guitars.
The traffic's hilarious, cars dance on a string,
And a cow flew by, oh, what joy it brings!

I harvest my laughter like crops in a field,
Finding the secrets that future will wield.
With sparkles and giggles floating around,
Who knew the cosmos had such a sound?

Colors of the Undiscovered

I painted tomorrow in shades of pure fun,
With stripes of bright jelly, and splatters of sun.
The canvas wobbled, laughed at my brush,
I swear it winked back in a carnival hush.

The hues of the future, a vibrant parade,
With dancing guitars in the grand charade.
My fridge is a rainbow, my sock drawer's a park,
Each color a dream, bursting to spark.

I asked a squirrel to pick my next shade,
He chose 'Invisible', for it's quite a trade.
When I tried to see it, I simply got lost,
In a whimsical world, where I paid the cost.

So let's brush the future with laughter and cheer,
Mix red with their wiggles and throw in some fear.
For in this big canvas, absurdity glows,
With colors undiscovered, anything goes!

Echoes of Undiscovered Paths

There's a door that squeaks quite loud,
Whispers jokes to the crowd.
It shows odd sights like a dog in a hat,
Wonders of future and where they are at.

Where will we go on this silly ride?
Through gardens with plants that giggle and glide.
Maybe visit a land of talking pies,
They all share secrets, and I hear their cries.

Revelation Through Panes

Through glass so clear, I peek and see,
A cat proposing to climb a tree.
An astronaut strumming a cosmic guitar,
While penguins play poker in a distant bazaar.

An owl in a suit, looks ready to dance,
With a twirl of the tail and a comical prance.
Each glance into the future brings laughter anew,
A clown on a rocket saying, "Huh, who knew?"

Shadows of What's Ahead

In shadows that giggle, I start to feel bright,
A chicken in boots is a peculiar sight.
A llama with sunglasses, relaxed in the sun,
Offers wise advice—"Life is just fun!"

What lies just beyond in the shadows we walk?
Maybe tacos that dance, or a fish that can talk.
Each layer reveals a new jolly crew,
With jokes that are cheesy, but oh, so true!

Views from the Threshold

Peeking from doorways, I shout with delight,
A squirrel on a skateboard zips past in full flight.
With gadgets so quirky, they spark and they beep,
While giraffes on a sofa enjoy their long sleep.

Oh, the silliness blossoms beyond that thin crest,
As unicorns toast to the very best quest.
They've got cupcakes and rainbows, a marvellous scene,
While I'm laughing aloud, "What does it all mean?"

Illuminated Futures

In a land of bright screens, all aglow,
We swipe left on choices, it's quite the show.
Pizza delivery drones hover like bees,
While cats rule the world with apparent ease.

Self-driving cars dance in festive parades,
Chasing squirrels and pizza, in hilarious raids.
Virtual reality turns life into play,
As we trade sunbathing for gaming all day.

With hats made of pixels and shoes made of sound,
Our future's a carnival, whirling 'round!
Texting our thoughts while munching on fries,
Tomorrow's a laugh—oh, what a surprise!

So let's all embrace this zany delight,
Where robots tell jokes and dance through the night.
Life's a giggle, a comedic spree,
In this quirky world, just dance like a bee!

A Glimpse Ahead

Peering through screens, oh what a sight,
Dogs in bow ties, taking flight!
People in suits made of rainbow bright,
Trading their woes for virtual delight.

In the future, hugs come in a can,
And coffee's brewed by a stylish man.
Umbrellas that tweet, oh isn't it grand,
While robots serve lunch with a well-timed hand.

Gravity's loose, as floats all around,
We ride on the clouds, floating off the ground.
With pogo-sticks powered by laughter and cheer,
Every day's silly, every moment's dear!

Let's play in the fun that is surely to come,
With echoes of giggles and beats of the drum.
A future of whimsy, endlessly bright,
Join the joyous dance, it's pure delight!

Portals of Awakening

Step through the portal, it's quite a thrill,
Where marshmallow trees grow on chocolate hill.
Socks that dance, and shoes with a beat,
Walking to work becomes quite the feat.

Time-traveling chefs make breakfast on Mars,
With pancakes shaped like funky guitars.
Every moment's a picture, every laugh's a song,
Come join the fun, where we all belong!

With robots that juggle and robots that sing,
A future where laughter is always the king.
So throw off your worries, let's cheer and let's play,
In this whimsical life, come what may!

Each door we open is filled with delight,
As penguins in tuxedos take flight into night.
Jump into joy, let your heart take a spin,
In this magical world, let the fun begin!

Catalysts of Change

Here comes the future, all quirky and bright,
Where toaster robots dance under moonlight.
Wearable food in fashionable wraps,
While youth with a giggle share viral snaps.

We've got flying cats and virtual pets,
All programming life with zero regrets.
Bananas with Wi-Fi, they surf with such flair,
Mimicking humans—a curious pair!

Our phones make us breakfast, our jackets tell jokes,
Life's a wide circus with giggles and pokes.
With every new gadget, the laughter expands,
As we swap all the serious for fun-making plans!

Embrace all the quirks, let the silliness reign,
In a world full of laughter, never feel pain.
The future's a carnival, bright and absurd,
When joy is the language, let's all be heard!

Scents of the Horizon's Bounty

The lemonade stand of tomorrow,
Squeezed by robots in a row.
Lemons roll in endless supply,
As lemonade rivers kiss the sky.

Flying cars with candy wheels,
Zooming past vineyards and peels.
Grapes dressed in sparkly hats,
Dance with the laughter of silly cats.

Gourmet pickles in rainbow jars,
Spread their taste beneath the stars.
They jam to tunes that never fade,
While cucumbers waltz, unafraid.

In fields where doughnuts grow like trees,
Honey bees trade jokes with the breeze.
The future smells like cotton candy,
As we sip joy that's never dandy.

Lenses of Infinite Dreams

See the world through goofy shades,
Where flying pigs stir up charades.
Unicorns prance on rainbows wide,
In a land where all can slide.

Silly hats that wiggle and sway,
Guide our futures on parade day.
Laughing clouds tickle our noses,
While marshmallow wonders floor our poses.

The telescope sees squirrels in suits,
Plotting joy in tiny pursuits.
Frogs in ties play leapfrog too,
In a dance as they pursue the blue.

With each glance, the future's bright,
Filled with whimsy and pure delight.
Join the fun, let laughter beam,
In this place of endless dream.

Pioneers of the Next Chapter

Cowboys ride on robots' backs,
Rustling laughter, cutting tracks.
Giddy-up into a world anew,
Where jellybeans grow like dew.

Fish in bow ties crack their jokes,
While squirrels tell tales of clever folks.
With spatulas, they lead a dance,
As pancakes swirl in a joyous trance.

Steampunk trains made of cheese,
Chug along with record ease.
Piglets in glasses, oh so wise,
Draw maps of chocolate, a sweet surprise.

In this land of playful schemes,
Everyone thrice dreams of ice creams.
Hold on tight as we explore,
The funny paths we can't ignore.

Tapestries of Surging Potential

Woven threads of giggles bright,
Stitch a future filled with light.
Mirthful patterns, twist and twirl,
In colorful designs that unfurl.

Kites made of pizza take to flight,
Chasing dreams in the soft twilight.
With each tug on the string held tight,
We'll explore realms of sheer delight.

Skateboards zoom with rainbow trails,
As wise old turtles spin their tales.
Doughnuts skip and dip around,
In this playground of joy abound.

We're artists painting with our smiles,
Creating futures full of miles.
In fields where chances bloom and play,
We dance our way into the day.

Translucent Tomorrows

Peeking through the glass, what do I see?
A cat in a tie sipping sweet iced tea.
Robots dancing, with style so grand,
Jellybean rainbows across the land.

Out of the fog, comes a pogo stick,
Riding the waves, performing a trick.
Flying goldfish with hats on their heads,
Tossing confetti, past waking beds.

Tomorrow's a circus, oh what a show!
Balloons that can giggle, and learn how to grow.
A squirrel on a skateboard zooms by,
Chewing his nut, shouting, "Who am I?"

With laughter and joy, we march on ahead,
Chasing our dreams through the clouds and thread.
In this strange realm where whimsy resides,
We float like balloons, where laughter abides.

A Canvas for Dreams

Brushstrokes of laughter paint the sky,
Where cupcakes and clouds quite often fly.
A canvas unrolled in a land so bright,
With marshmallow suns that glow through the night.

Painting with giggles, dipped in pure cheer,
Imaginations roaming, free from all fear.
Pigs in pajamas spin cartwheels with glee,
While unicorns sip on warm cups of tea.

Our dreams are the colors, wild and bold,
With silver linings made out of gold.
In this art-filled world, everything's whacky,
Elephants dance, and the owls are quite snappy.

So let's splash our wishes on the nighttime sky,
With splatters of joy that just can't run dry.
With laughter as paint, we'll keep it aglow,
In the gallery of dreams, where fun always flows.

Echoes of the Unimagined

In the hall of echoes, strange voices play,
A goat in glasses says, "Hey, let's sway!"
Sounds of laughter bounce off the wall,
As walruses juggle, oh what a ball!

Twirling through whispers of worlds we've not seen,
A penguin in tuxedo, mighty and keen.
He nods to the giraffe, who's painting his nails,
While kittens on bicycles plot grander trails.

In the silence of dreams, the funny takes flight,
With echoes of trivia, odd facts delight.
Jelly beans whisper of futures so wild,
As teddy bears serenade every child.

With chortles and chuckles filling the air,
The unimagined holds wonders to share.
So let's find our voices in this curious place,
And revel together in laughter's embrace.

Lighthouses for Lost Dreams

Shining bright on shores where wishes drift,
Lighthouses dance, giving spirits a lift.
With beams of humor guiding the way,
Through fog and mirth, they sway and play.

A lighthouse made of candy, shining sweet,
With chocolate waves that it playfully greets.
Gummy bear sailors, twirling with glee,
While marshmallow clouds roll in from the sea.

Stumbling flamingos shout, "Ahoy matey!"
While high-fiving crabs, feeling all hasty.
In the distance, a whale sings a tune,
Of lost dreams returning, like night turns to noon.

So let's sail the seas of the whimsically free,
With lighthouses glowing, come dance with me!
For in every beacon, a giggle awaits,
A harbor of laughter, where fun celebrates.

Mosaics of the Possible

In a world of pixelated dreams,
I tripped on a tile, or so it seems.
Each shard a laugh, a wacky spin,
In this glassy space, let the fun begin.

A cat in a hat on a flying board,
With jellybeans flying, what a reward!
Here, jellyfish dance in roller skates,
While talking toasters serve up the fates.

A fish in a tux holds a crumpet tight,
He winks at the moon, it's quite a sight.
A toaster sings opera, the screens alight,
Mosaics of life, such a silly delight!

The future's a joke, the punchline is clear,
A giggle, a chuckle, it's drawing near.
So paint your path with colors so bold,
For laughter unlocks what the fables have told.

Foresight Through Clearness

With goggles of laughter, I peek through the haze,
Seeing robots doing the funky maze.
A parrot in glasses reads the news,
While cows in tutu's tap dance with shoes.

Chickens on bikes zoom past with glee,
"Why did the chicken?" they ask with a plea.
The answer's a riddle, held tight in the air,
While ducks in bowties float without a care.

I check my crystal ball with a grin,
It shows my neighbor growing a leaf-blower fin.
Predicting the future? Now that's a hoot,
When cats start knitting in old-fashioned suits!

So let's toast to the new, the bright, and the clear,
With foresight like this, there's nothing to fear.
We'll dance through the ages, no need for a plan,
In this wild, wacky future, we'll all be a fan!

Patterns of Tomorrow's Weave

In a fabric of dreams that tickle and tease,
A squirrel with a monocle hops through the trees.
Threads of spaghetti and cupcakes galore,
We weave patterns of joy, who could ask for more?

A quilt of the future, stitched with delight,
With unicorns knitting by moon's gentle light.
The fabric tells tales of dance and of cheer,
Of waffle wars fought in the backyard and near.

Patterns ember like fireworks at night,
A llama in overalls, what a silly sight!
Each stitch a reminder, laughter's our thread,
As we sew our tomorrows, letting joy spread.

So wear your odd socks, embrace the strange spin,
For tomorrow's a tapestry where fun can begin.
With laughter as needles, let's craft and believe,
In patterns of joy, let's all take our leave!

A Map to What Lies Ahead

Here's a map made of cheese with a sprinkle of fun,
Each x marks the spot for a wild roller run.
Follow the turtles in tutus and ties,
To a glorious land where the giggles arise.

Across rivers of soda, and valleys of cake,
We'll leap over puddles, make no mistake.
Where the clouds are made of pink cotton candy,
And the sun's a big smile, it's all feeling dandy.

The paths twist and turn like a wiggly worm,
Spilling out laughter, let joy be the firm.
So pick up your compass, toss out the dread,
As we sail into mischief, with giggles instead.

This map is a treasure, for fun we will tread,
To mysteries waiting, let's follow the thread.
For what truly lies ahead? A world full of cheer,
With companions of whimsy, there's nothing to fear!

Visions Taken Flight

Through panes of glass, we see the show,
With popcorn close, watch dreams aglow.
A bird in socks, a cat in a hat,
Life's quirks unfold and we all have a spat.

Chasing rainbows on roller blades,
Unicorns dressed in silly parades.
A jester juggles on a cloud nine,
As we laugh and sip sparkling brine.

Mirrors reflect what we hope to see,
A giraffe playing chess beneath a tree.
With each goofy glance, a chance to smile,
Future shenanigans are worth the while!

So let's all dance on this wobbly floor,
With robots serving snacks, who could want more?
What's next on the list? A martian band?
Just hold on tight, and let fun expand!

Archways to New Realities

Step through the arch made of candy canes,
Where squirrels ride bicycles and sing refrains.
A ceiling of cupcakes, a floor of fondue,
In this silly realm, who needs to be blue?

A walrus in glasses tries to do a jig,
While dancing on top of a chocolate pig.
The seasons reverse, snow melts into toast,
Life's simply grand, let's laugh and boast!

Bouncing clouds sing soft lullabies,
As fish in top hats pirouette and rise.
Everyone's invited, just bring your flair,
And don't forget that sprightly air!

We twirl and we swirl in magical light,
In this wacky place where odd feels right.
So, join the circus on this sunny stage,
Where fun is the trend, let us all engage!

Skylines Beyond the Current

Look at the skyline with wobbly touches,
Where giraffes dance tango, and laughter clutches.
Kites made of pizza swirl in the breeze,
While cows in pajamas climb up with ease.

Time-traveling hotdogs roam the street,
In shoes made of marshmallows, oh what a treat!
With dolphins on skateboards zooming by fast,
Each day is a carnival, full of contrast.

A fireworks show made of jelly beans,
Where laughter erupts, lifting all our means.
Let's toast with soda, on clouds of whipped cream,
In this zany world, live your wildest dream!

As the sun sets with a wink and a nod,
We'll revel in quirks, give plain some facade.
So grab a balloon and let's float above,
In a world painted solely with giggles and love.

Embracing the Unto Yet

In the great unknown, a circus appears,
With elephants prancing and juggling their fears.
They wear little hats as they spin and twirl,
In a laugh-a-lot world, where pranks unfurl.

The sun smiles wide, as the moon starts to wink,
In a hiccuping river, where giggles sink.
Dancing with dolphins on pogo sticks,
What's life without laughter? Just a few tricks!

Riding a turtle through cotton candy skies,
With flower petal confetti that giggles and flies.
A cake for a chair, come sit and have fun,
In this land of silliness, worry's outdone.

So clink your glass with the fairy next door,
As we celebrate life like never before.
With joy in our hearts and a skip in our step,
We embrace all the wild, with laughter adept!

www.ingramcontent.com/pod-product-compliance
Lightning Source LLC
Chambersburg PA
CBHW070305120526
44590CB00017B/2574